How to Keep the Republic:

What you Need to Know

John Chambers

Copyright © 2005, 2010, 2018 John Chambers
All Rights Reserved

www.ItsYourConstitution.com

ISBN-13: 978-1720780403
ISBN-10: 1720780404

Dedicated to You
who will Keep the Republic
for our Grandchildren

At the conclusion of the Constitutional Convention in 1787, Mrs. Eliza (Elizabeth) Powel asked Ben Franklin what form of government the convention had cooked up. Franklin famously answered: "We have given you a republic, if you can keep it."

"Keeping it" is the job of every citizen. Like any job, it takes information and figuring out what is important and what is not.

Every day, we wear many hats. We wear our parent hat one minute, our good neighbor hat the next, and when we go to work there are a whole new set of hats.

What about your Citizen hat? You have one, and you do it the best you can with the information you have.

This little booklet gives you all the information you need to *operate* as a citizen. Study this booklet well. Read each section, starting with the definitions of the key terms, a fun exercise even if you think you already know what a word means. Maybe you do, but you may find an unexpected nugget here and there. Then read the section and answer the questions at the end.

When satisfied you know that section, go on to the next. No skipping. They build on each other.

The more you work at it, the more effective you will be.

How to Keep the Republic:
What you need to Know

Contents

What is a Citizen Hat?

HOW WOULD YOU KNOW IF YOU FOUND ONE? THIS SECTION DESCRIBES WHAT IT IS, AND WHAT IT ISN'T.

KEY TERMS:

Citizen is "a person owing loyalty to and entitled … to the protection of a state or nation" says the *American Heritage Dictionary*. Some would say a citizen is anyone who lives in a state or nation, but more properly, the person must be *loyal* to it as well.

The ancient origin of the word is the same as *city* – think of a <u>cit</u>y-den<u>izen</u> = *citizen*. Most any ancient city in which a person would have boasted citizenship was a Democracy such as Athens, or a Republic such as Rome. The "citizen" participated in the decision-making (**politics***) of the city. Therefore, the term "citizen" implies one who participates, or is allowed to participate, in the **government** of the city. As a member of a political community, a citizen has a voice in the government.

---

* Words in **bold** in the definition are defined in list of KEY TERMS. **Politics** is defines on page 9 below.

Hat is, of course, a covering for a head, but also is "a role or office symbolized by or as if by the wearing" of a hat, says the *American Heritage Dictionary.* It is the **rights, duties** and **responsibilities** that go along with a job. A nurse's cap makes a person recognizable as a Nurse. The same is true of a soldier, sailor, bishop, railway conductor, and so on. If a person in a nurse's hat wants to take your blood pressure, you would not object because you know that is part of her job. It is her hat.

Civics is the study of the **rights, duties** and **responsibilities** (the **hat**) of a **citizen.**

Rights and "powers" are abilities. A right is an ability of a person while a "power" is an ability of a **government.** A person may have a *right* to speak while a government has a *power* to tax.

According to *American Heritage Dictionary*, a right is "that which is just, morally good, legal, proper, or fitting" or "something that is due to a person or governmental body by law, tradition, or nature."

A person wearing a **hat** uses rights to carry out his **responsibilities** and **duties**. Continuing the car and driver analogy, a person has the right to drive on any public road. He has that right because he wears the hat, performs the duties, which means no one will stop him, and the responsibilities as well so he has the strength and capacity to take the action.

Duties are those actions that a person has agreed to do.

A duty is "an obligation assumed (as by contract) or imposed by law," says *Merriam-Webster's Dictionary of Law*. It is an obligation to others.

For instance, everyone expects the driver of a car to obey traffic signals. When he sits behind the wheel, he puts on the **hat** of a driver and agrees to stop at red lights. It is his duty.

He chooses to be a driver. With that comes a duty to not harm others. (A "duty" is also a tax on an item coming into the community from a foreign place.)

Responsibilities are those actions a person takes to forward a purpose. Many dictionaries confuse "responsibility" with **"duty,"** but they are different. A driver, for instance, has a *duty* to stop at a stoplight but he has the *responsibility* to take care of his car. Getting a tune-up is not a duty, but if the driver wants to drive, he'll get it done.

"Taking responsibility" means recognizing that fulfilling your purpose depends on your own action. Some say it is "just the right thing to do." *The Destiny of Freedom* defines responsibility as "the willingness to embrace a purpose." An action can be both a duty and a responsibility.

Liberty, according to *Merriam-Webster's Dictionary of Law* is "freedom from external (as governmental) restraint, compulsion, or interference." It is freedom in a governmental setting. "Freedom" is the ability to choose. For instance, a person has a freedom to buy one car or another. When it is said that a person is "at liberty" to buy one car or another, it suggests the government is not going to interfere with his choice. Liberty means the condition of a person who is not restrained by a government.

But it means more than that.

Freedom is "you can do anything you want." *Liberty* is "you can do anything you want as long as you do not violate the rights of others."

Government steps in when a person violates the rights of others. **Rights** can only be exercised in liberty.

Politics, according to *Webster's* (1924), is "the theory and practice of managing or directing the affairs of [state]." Mainly applied to nations and states, the term is also used to describe attempts to influence decisions in other settings, such as "office politics." It is the theory and practice of making decisions.

Because **government** does use force, some say that "political science" is the study of the acquisition and use of force to impose one's will. More broadly, politics is how decisions are made. A decision made using the "political process" is a "policy." The term "politics" comes from the Greek word *polis*, which means "city" (see **citizen**).

Government is the "exercise of authority in a political unit," says the *American Heritage Dictionary*. It is the collection of institutions (institution: a way of doing things) that steers a society. Society allows government, above all other institutions, to use force. As George Washington observed, "Government is not reason. Government is not eloquence. It is force."

How government makes decisions is called **politics**. The institutions and their relationships are the **constitution** of the government. "Government" is also the study of governance.

Governance means the act or fact of guiding and/or controlling the community. It is "how to govern." The word comes from an ancient Greek word that meant "to steer."

Constitution is the "the composition or structure of something" (*American Heritage Dictionary*). For a **government**, it is the rules, written or not, that define the institutions (and the relationships between those institutions) that form the government. A Constitution can grow over time or can be determined before the government begins. The document known as "The Constitution of the United States" defines the institutions that constitute the U.S. government.

The Importance of the Citizen

For most of history in most parts of the world, the job of a Citizen was to *obey*. The people were owned by the government, whether a King, Emperor, Shogun, Czar, or Pharaoh.

In a few places during unique times, the Citizen owned the government. The hat of a Citizen was to make the government obey. Traditionally, the practice started in Athens 2400 years ago, went to Rome 2200 years ago and on to England and America.

Lesser known places and times, the Iroquois 300 years ago, Florence off and on 500 years ago and Switzerland for the last 500 years, can also be of interest.

Each of these political communities developed ways of doing things (institutions) in which the citizens governed themselves. For instance, the Council of Women was the only group allowed to send the Iroquois Nation to War.

In the 18th century, the Founding Fathers of the United States were familiar with the subject of Governance through the examples of each of the communities above (Switzerland was even known as a "Sister Republic"). The United States would survive, but only if, as in Switzerland, each citizen wore his Hat as a Citizen.

Because our job as citizens is to make the government obey, the subject of "civics" must cover more than the institutions of our government – how a bill becomes Law and that the President is the Commander-in-Chief. Civics must also include the principles of Good Governance. By analogy, a parent not only needs to know what the children *are* doing, but what they *should* be doing. If citizens do not know what constitutes good governance, the institutions that we call government may (and the cynical would say, "Probably will") govern badly and we would not know. Not knowing, we would not demand the government to change.

For instance, some say the jury system should be abandoned. Outrageous billion-dollar jury awards and idiotic juror antics in high-profile cases might convince a citizen to agree. But one of the maxims of Good Governance could be stated as "Government action must conform to the Customs of the People." In a jury system, if a law does not conform to the customs of the people, a jury keeps the government in line. For instance, the recent controversy (United States, 2005) over Eminent Domain would be solved if Juries, as guaranteed in the 7th Amendment to the Constitution, were allowed to assign "just compensation" as guaranteed in the 5th Amendment. The jury system ensures that governmental actions conform to the Customs of the People.

In a Republic (frequently called a "Western Democracy" or "Democracy" for short) like the Swiss or the United States, the citizens own the government. Some publications will tell you how to get benefits from the government. There is nothing wrong with that as long as you do not become dependent on the government. Then the government owns you. A Citizen Hat would tell you how to own the government.

This is our government. It is okay to own it.

Answer These Questions

1. **What reason(s) do *you* have to become more "hatted" (know your job) as a citizen?** (If you cannot think of a reason, please do not subject yourself to the stress of reading something that does not interest you. You may pick it up later when it does interest you.)

2. **What might happen if you don't?**

Is Government Necessary?

THIS SECTION LOOKS AT WHY WE WOULD WANT ONE.

KEY TERMS:

Purpose means what is intended, the reason something is done, or the use of something. As a legal term, it is "*specifically* : the … activity in which a corporation is chartered to engage" according to the *Merriam-Webster Dictionary of Law*. *If the **corporation** is doing things it was not **chartered** to do, it is no longer following its purpose.*

Corporation is a body (from the Latin *corpus*: "body") created by a **sovereign** to do particular actions. Most large businesses are corporations chartered by states. The business is "incorporated in California" (or Florida, Delaware, Oregon, etc.). It has papers from the state saying it engages in such-and-such business.   The Federal Government, by "an Act of Congress," charters some corporations, such as the Federal Reserve. Queen Elizabeth I chartered the British East India Company in 1600.

Sovereign means the person or persons with the final say in a political community. A sovereign "exercises supreme, permanent authority, especially in a nation or other governmental unit" says the *American Heritage Dictionary*. Whether a king or queen, or "a national governing council or committee" such as Congress, the sovereign is the undisputed ruler. In a democracy, the citizenry are sovereign. In a republic, they are sovereign within Constitutional limits. The word comes from the Latin *super*, which means "above."

Charter is the act of, or the document produced by, a **sovereign** when giving permission for a **corporation** to exist. It usually states why the sovereign is granting the new body its powers and then lists the powers so granted. For instance, the document known as the Constitution of the United States is a charter. The charter is from the **sovereign** people and states, united, in America. The charter specifies why they are granting powers to a new **corporation** and then states those powers and limitations on those powers. The word comes from the Latin for "sheet of paper."

The Purpose of Government

A government does for you the things you cannot do yourself. As Thomas Paine observed in *Common Sense*, it is the Constitution of the People rather than the Constitution of the Government that determines how iron-fisted the government will be.

In a land of people who want government to do everything for them, they will become dependent on government. No matter how honorable the original founding of the county, people serving in the government will eventually take advantage of that dependency and you will have an oppressive government.

In a land of self-reliant people, the government will hardly be noticed.

The government steers the group. It is the rudder that directs the ship. The captain of the ship may tell the helmsman how to move the rudder, or the crew may vote on their direction, but the rudder is the mechanism that turns the ship of state.

Government is the mechanism used by a sovereign to do things the sovereign cannot do alone.

The government administers (manages the execution of, from the Latin *ministr-* "servant") the activities of the community, moving the community toward that which is most valued by the sovereign.

The government of an association of petroleum producers will probably administer the association to maximize oil profits.

The government of a family will take actions to ensure the children grow into responsible adults.

The government of a Democracy will ensure that every voice is heard.

The government of a Republic may regard liberty as "the highest political end" (as in 19th century Britain) or may work for the increase of its influence (as in Rome), but whatever goal is set, it will limit government to that end.

For British colonials in America in 1776, the purpose of government was clear. First, it was self-evident that all men had powers and abilities (rights) that could not be separated from them. Life and liberty were part of a person. Without life, without liberty, a person was, well, no longer a person.

It was also self-evident that men were not angels. There were (and are) those who wish, by force, to take from others that which is not theirs to take. To protect the unalienable rights from undue stress, the Declaration of Independence says, "governments are instituted among men." To them, the purpose was clear: government protects honest folks from thugs.

A dozen years later, after a war threw off the thugs of the former regime, these same people chartered a new government. In the introduction to the charter (its "preamble"), they named the exact purpose of the new corporation. Briefly, the purpose of the Government of the United States is to:

- **Form a more perfect union** because the 13 states needed to work together. Some distrusted the others. They had different forms of money. Travel and trade, state to state, was difficult. They felt the need to work together in harmony.

- **Establish justice** because no person is safe if thugs can terrorize honest folks. After forming a better union, the new government was to make the people safe in life and liberty by assuring that the bad guy gets his just penalty and the honest one his proper reward.

- **Insure domestic tranquility** because riots had recently broken out. Life, liberty and the pursuit of happiness cannot thrive in chaos. Justice will go a long way toward insuring tranquility, but the new government may need to take additional steps.

- **Provide for the common defense** because each state had its own militia but armies operate best under a central command. Additionally, the armies of Spain might think twice about invading Georgia if they knew they would be fighting Massachusetts as well. A united front does give an enemy pause. After domestic tranquility is insured, it needs to be safeguarded from foreign invasion.

- **Promote the general welfare** because governments can do some things better than private enterprise. *General* welfare means "good for everyone." Courts, with the power to enforce decisions (assuming just decisions) are good for everyone. Protecting (with bayonets and jail-time if necessary) copyrights and patents promote creativity and industriousness. That is good for everyone. Common money and standard weights and measures enhance trade, good for everyone. A country, tranquil at home and safe from invasion, can, with good governance, increase the welfare of *all* the people.

- **Secure the blessings of liberty to ourselves and our posterity** because liberty can be won in a war but a people must also win the peace. This government being chartered by the people of the several states was to ensure that future generations enjoyed tranquility, safety and welfare into the future.

The job of a Citizen is to watch, verify and demand that the government remain true to its purpose.

Answer These Questions

1. What purpose(s) do you want your government to serve?

2. What, if anything, do you do now to ensure that it follows that purpose?

Forms of Government

ASSUMING WE HAVE A PURPOSE FOR A GOVERNMENT,
WHAT FORM SHOULD IT TAKE? THIS SECTION LOOKS AT THE
CLASSICAL FORMS AVAILABLE.

KEY TERMS:

Monarchy is rule by one person "usually for life and by hereditary right" according to the *American Heritage Dictionary*. The essence of monarchy is "one ruler" whether a hereditary king, a pirate captain, or an elected president. This has the advantage of being fast. Decisions are made quickly and the ship of state turns on a dime. BUT it has the disadvantage that the monarch can turn into a murderous dictator. Removing him from power can take heroic effort. The word comes from the Greek *mono-*, only or single; and *-archy*, ruler

Aristocracy, says the *American Heritage Dictionary*, is "government by the citizens deemed to be best qualified to lead." The best can be those with the most land, or the best education, or the elders of the tribe. The best are always a minority. The minority of the "best" will take care of the others (the majority) who are less able. The advantage is that everyone is cared for. Further, no aristocrat will become a murderous dictator. His colleagues will hold him in check. BUT the disadvantage is that "the best" might make decisions without regard for the majority. Restoring the rights of the majority takes a Reign of Terror. From the Greek *aristo-*, the best; and -*cracy*, strength or power.

Democracy is generally said to be "government by the people, exercised either directly or through elected representatives" but in its simplicity, means "majority rule" (both definitions from the *American Heritage Dictionary*). The advantage is that every voice is heard. To have every voice heard was the hope of Pericles, which hope started the Golden Age of Greece and has been a defining factor of Western Civilization ever since. BUT the disadvantage is that the majority is always average, never above-average. Democracy tends toward mediocrity. From the Greek *demo-*, people; and -*cracy*, strength or power.

What is a Republic?

Most dictionaries define a "republic" as a form of government headed usually by a president who is not a monarch and that "supreme power lies in a body of citizens who can elect people to represent them." But that is almost identical to the definition of Democracy above.

Indeed, our form of government is often called a "Democracy." Is our government a Democracy or a Republic? Is there a difference?

The difference was first mentioned by Aristotle in his *Politics*. He said there were three basic forms of government. There was rule by one person (a Monarchy), rule by a minority (an Aristocracy), or rule by the majority, a Democracy.

In each of those, rules can made for the benefit of the common good, or for selfish reasons.

Six forms of government. The peculiarity was that the majority rule in his experience had never worked out for the common good. It always had to have an agreed-upon structure, what he called a "Constitutional Polity."

Polity has a number of meanings but the one that applies is "an organized society." Society has a number of parts. It is a mix-and-match of a single ruler, different minorities or "interests", even large "minorities." Its "constitution" describes the parts and

FOR THE BENEFIT OF	Single Ruler	A Minority	Rule by Many
The Common Good	Monarchy	Aristocracy	Constitutional Polity
Selfish Interest	Tyranny	Oligarchy	Democracy

how they fit together.

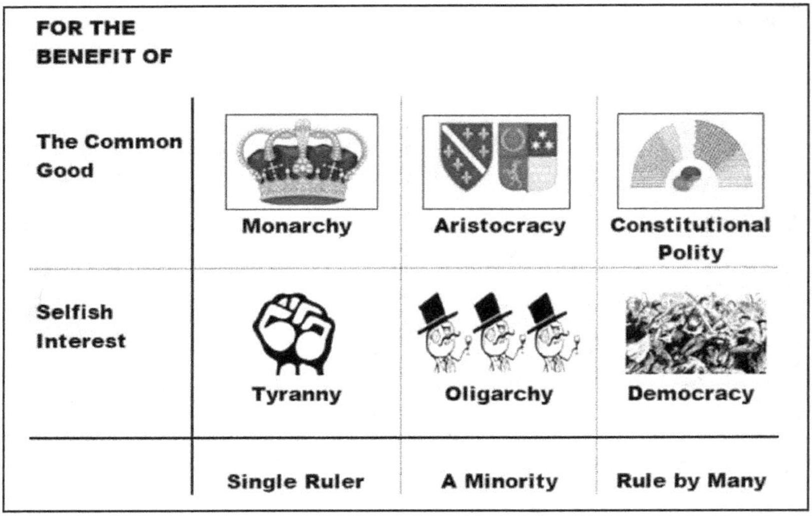

About 150 years after Aristotle, Rome conquered the Greek civilization and Polybius, a Greek historian, became a tutor to young Roman gentlemen.

The Roman government was a "Constitutional Polity" they called *Res Publica* (The People's Thing). Polybius studied and taught the forms of government, making slight change to Aristotle's initial classification.

What we call a *republic* is a constitutional polity. It is composed of the three basic forms of government. Those three "branches" have relationships to each other defined by the Constitution of the Polity.

If will have a Democratic element.

It will have a Monarch-single-leader element.

It will have an Aristocratic element.

All elements will work together, and all must agree (somewhat) with the others for a law to take effect.

A government "steers" a group, as mentioned in a previous section. The purpose of the society, what it considers valuable, tells the government where to steer. The constitution tells it *how* to steer. How to steer depends on the composition of the group.

The Cycle of Governments

Polybius noticed these three forms of government cycle from one form to another, each form starting well, degrading, and finally being replaced by another. His observations were later confirmed and refined by at least one historian (see *Polybius* in **Further Reading** section).

Briefly, the cycle works as follows, beginning with a democracy.

(1) In a democracy, every voice contributes to society and is heard. To maintain that, the culture must give to each voice enough information to make it an educated and informed voice. Additionally, each voice must maintain a level of ethics and responsibility sufficient to consider not only its own wellbeing but also the welfare of others. That is to say, each citizen wears his hat.

Well, that is how it *should* work. At the start, it does.

(2) But a time comes when citizens stop wearing their hats. What causes this is not easy to see because

those who cause it do not want to be seen. Criminal thugs who wish to hide their antisocial crimes misdirect attention and give "others" a bad name.

Whether you are "conservative" or "liberal," you can think of an example of an antisocial person – someone who tells you everything is bad and "others" have caused it. Antisocial individuals suppress education. They confuse and upset the average person into no longer caring about others.

As mentioned above, the disadvantage of a democracy is that the majority tends toward mediocrity. The Above-average are, by definition, a minority. The majority, denied education and spurred by the antisocial to despise "others" and envy a brilliant or talented minority, are tricked into voting to destroy them.

(3) Without its best and brightest, the society falls apart. When it does fall apart, the brilliant and talented will find a way to take over, overtly or covertly. The ensuing government will be a monarchy or aristocracy. It works for a while.

(4) It does not take long for the ensuing monarch or aristocracy to fall prey to antisocial individuals. They oppress the majority. Finally, (5), the majority revolt and install a democracy. It has been said that the entire cycle takes about 200 years.

The common failing of (a) monarchy, (b) aristocracy and (c) democracy is that the ruling entity *can* gain unlimited control, and under the influence of the antisocial, it *will* gain Unlimited Power.

The Mixed Government

The Constitutional Polity is called a "Mixed" government. The "Mixed" government has elements of each of the other three. The "monarchical" element is usually in charge of the army and day-to-day administration of government functions. The "aristocratic" element is usually in charge of the courts and/or the purse while the "democratic" element usually has the power to adopt laws, often with the agreement of the other two "branches" of the government.

If the "monarch" tries to grab too much power, the other branches will withhold his pay or otherwise check him. If the "aristocrats" try to grab all the power, the monarch and democrats can use the army against them. If the democrats become a mob, the army and the courts will stop them.

The purpose of a mixed government is to limit the power of government.

No matter the composition of the society or where that society wants to go, the people realize they can only thrive if the government is limited.

A Republic is a mixed government. In the United States Republic, the President is monarchical; Congress is democratic; the Judiciary is aristocratic. Much more could be said to detail how these three branches limit the powers of the others. It is clear from reading the *Federalist Papers* (see **Further Reading**), essays written to urge the adoption of the U. S. Constitution, that the intent of the Constitution was to create a mixed government, a republic. The purpose was to have a government run by laws that maximized liberty by limiting the power of the Government.

Everyone but the very antisocial will agree that a society is best if each individual is "capable of caring for himself and family, [able to] help and be helped by his neighbors" with "a level of ethics and responsibility sufficient to consider not only [his] own wellbeing but also the welfare of others."

Everyone but the very antisocial wants to live in a democracy. The antisocial, however, work hard to make people dependent, incapable and unwilling to consider the welfare of others. These individuals hope to create a society needing an aristocracy. The antisocial wants to be recognized as "the best," of course, and *become* the Aristocracy.

Some, commonly called "conservatives," say that the aristocracy is "big government" or the "welfare state" which wants to victimize everyone by reducing all to government dependency. Others, commonly called "liberals," say that the aristocracy is "corporate interests" or the "religious Right." They see that ownership of property and a belief in God oppresses and victimizes others. Both want a real democracy but sense an unseen aristocracy.

When the truly antisocial individuals are identified, on that day both liberal and conservative folk will suddenly find there are fewer victims.

On that day, democracy will work.

Until then, we have to settle for a Constitutional Polity, a Republic.

The peculiarity of a Republic is that it is not a natural form of government. As natural as rain, a group of people will choose to be governed by a Monarchy, an Aristocracy, or a Democracy.

If most of the people in a group cannot take care of themselves, then those who can take care of them will, and an Aristocracy will arise whether anyone wants it or not.

Similarly, if everyone in the group is headed in the same direction, a monarchy will naturally arise. The group can't help it.   The people will choose someone to lead them.

Finally, if everyone in a group can take care of himself and also watch out for the well-being of others, they will form a democracy.   It will arise without anyone suggesting it. It just happens.

A Republic is not natural. It is constructed; it is man-made. The constant struggle in a Republic is to not decay into one of the Natural forms.

The People's Thing, to serve the people, requires constant attention from the people.

Recall the famous words of Benjamin Franklin. Directly after the Constitutional Convention, the story goes, Mrs. Elizabeth Powel anxiously asked Franklin: "Well Doctor, what have you given us, a republic or a monarchy?"

"A republic," answered Franklin, "if you can keep it."

Answer These Questions

1. Would you like to live in a Democracy?

2. Do you live in a Republic, or a Democracy?

3. What do *you* think is the main problem facing us?

4. Do you think there might be unseen antisocial individuals causing that problem? If so, who do you think those individuals might be?

Powers (Tools) of Government

HOW DOES A GOVERNMENT ACHIEVE ITS PURPOSE? THIS SECTION LOOKS AT HOW A GOVERNMENT DOES ITS JOB.

KEY TERMS:

Authority is the ability to make decisions or give orders. In *Merriam-Webster's Dictionary of Law*, it is "a power to act esp. over others" or "the power to act that is officially or formally granted". *It also implies the responsibility for the decisions and actions made. It comes from the Latin for "creator."*

Legitimate is to be "in accordance [agreement] with established or accepted patterns and standards" says the *American Heritage Dictionary while Merriam-Webster's Dictionary of Law* adds that it is "being in accordance with law or with established legal forms and requirements." Something is "legitimate" if it is generally agreed that it is the way it should be. Anything legitimate will be found to agree with **the "civil religion."** The word comes from the Latin *lex*, meaning **"law."**

Civil Religion is, according to the *Encyclopedia of*

Religion and Society, "the transcendent universal religion of the nation". It is the values, the worldview, the self-evident assumptions, that everyone in the society believes, no matter if it is Christian, Buddhist, Humanist, or anything else.

Law is a "rule of conduct or procedure" dictionaries seem to agree. A law describes an act that one must do or must not do, and how the doing (or not doing) of the act will be **enforced**. Most laws will define a **tax**, a **benefit**, a **crime** or a **punishment**. It is a **rule** that has been laid down by a recognized authority. It is *not* something made up on the spur-of-the-moment. "Legislation" is the act or fact of making a law. The word comes from Old Norse *lag*, which meant "that which is laid down."

Rule is a "prescribed direction of conduct" or "guide of conduct" depending on the dictionary. It is also how rules are made. For instance, "rule of law" means that the rules are defined by prior agreements (**laws**) while "rule of men" means that the rules are made up on the spur-of-the-moment at the whim of whoever is in power. It is from the Latin *regula*, meaning "rod" or "principle" which is also the root of "regular."

Enforce is to demand conduct, by the use of force if necessary. The word comes from "force" which comes from Latin *fortis*, "strong."

Tax is the act or fact of a "contribution for the support of a government required of persons, groups, or businesses within the domain of that government" according to the *American Heritage Dictionary*. Some **laws** define what taxes are to be paid by whom, and the methods of **enforcing** their payment. The word comes from Latin "to asses (or fix) the value of" from earlier Latin "to touch."

Benefit is something that gives an advantage to, or is a payment to, a person. A **law** can define a benefit to be given to a person or class of persons, who those persons are, and the method of payment. It is from the Latin "to do a service."

Crime is "an unjust, senseless, or disgraceful act or condition" says the *American Heritage Dictionary*. A **law** can define an act or condition as "a crime" in which case the act or condition becomes "a violation of the law," another definition of crime. The word comes from the Latin crimen, "crime."

Punishment is, the *American Heritage Dictionary* says, "a penalty imposed for wrongdoing."

How Government Does its Job

A government does its job by making rules and getting them followed. A rule is made and enforced to achieve some purpose. For instance, in a family, to achieve the purpose of a livable environment, the trash must be taken out.

If no one "takes responsibility" for the trash-removal hat, the government (let's call her "Mom") steps in and a rule is made about who takes out the trash (let's call him "Joey"). We can all hope that Joey will do the right thing ("takes responsibility"), but if Joey refuses to follow the rule, Mom has to step in and enforce the rule. If she doesn't, that family may have a place to live, but it would hardly be called a "home."

In a society, whether a family or a nation, the government, and only the government, is allowed to use force to achieve its purpose. If any other person or group asserts it has the authority to enforce rules it concocts, the real government will use its force to suppress the illegitimate "authority."

To enforce its rules, a government must be seen as legitimate. According to German political economist Max Weber, founder of modern sociology, legitimate authority can be gained through three means:

- long-standing tradition ("that's the way it has always been"),

- inspirational charisma ("people follow him without knowing why"), or
- legal rationality ("the law makes sense").

The essence of legitimacy is agreement. Most observers will note that, in addition to Weber's methods above, grudging agreement can be gained through

- brute force ("agree or be hurt") or
- bribery ("agree and be paid").

However it happens, legitimacy means folks are willing to support enforcement of the rules.

The source of legitimacy is fluid. For instance, a charismatic leader, after a number of years, could gain legitimacy through "tradition." Equally, a legal-rational government might be taken over by a brute-force cabal or charismatic bribery. When it does, its legitimacy will be questioned.

Most modern governments hope to gain agreement through legal-rational legitimacy. Most complaints you have about your government are that some action (or inaction) was either (1) not according to law or (2) made no sense.

Rational-legal governments gain agreement through laws that reflect good governance. Good laws increase legitimacy.

For instance, laws that define crimes will be supported if folks view those acts as despicable. A law defining a punishment will be supported if folks view the punishment as fitting the crime (just). Laws that raise or collect taxes will be supported if folks believe the money is being used for worthwhile purposes. Laws that grant benefits will be supported, again, if folks believe the purpose is worthy.

Taxes may not be agreeable but how the money is spent has everything to do with legitimacy. When the government spends its money on programs contrary to the purposes of the society it governs (the rudder is steering the ship in the wrong direction), people may not know exactly what is wrong, but are disinclined to follow. Money represents value. Most revolts over "taxes" were really revolutions over values – the money was spent poorly.

Values come from a worldview of Who or What Rules The Universe and How Things Should Be. Everyone, whether Hindu, Christian, Muslim, Materialist, Marxist, has values based on his worldview, also known as Religion.

Any rule designed to sway a person's worldview is not Good Governance. By definition, a rule of government may require enforcement. Enforcement of a worldview cannot be accomplished. No matter how much force the government (or anyone) applies, a person's worldview will not change. The person may say he has changed. He becomes a beaten dog and gives in to pressure but any law designed to sway a person's worldview can only lead to degradation. That is not Good Governance.

The "Civil Religion" of a society is the values, the worldview, the self-evident assumptions that everyone in the society believes. The values are not enforced. They just are. For instance, in the United States, anyone will agree that "you can do anything you want as long as it does not hurt anyone else." One who does not hold that view is looked upon as very odd. Any law enforced in the United States must conform to that maxim or it will be viewed as illegitimate.

Those who do not hold that view, such as a rapist (who believes he has a right to rape whether it hurts another or not), will complain that the law is trying to force a "no-rape" worldview on him. He would be right. He would also be laughed out of society and locked up.

Taxes, as said before, rarely affect legitimacy. Much more can be said on this subject (see *For Good and Evil* in **Further Reading**), especially when taxes are used to change conduct rather than raise revenue, as is frequently suspected with the US Internal Revenue Code.

Nevertheless, legitimacy is affected much more by how the money is spent – benefits granted. Benefits might be tax-breaks for businesses that do what the government wants. Benefits might be payments or special services to those who need it. As long as the benefits and their administration conform to the "Civil Religion" they will be legitimate even if not within the strict purpose of the government. They will be allowed under a "liberal" or loose construction of the purpose of the constitution. On the other hand, unrest and eventual revolution occurs when the government violates the values of the People too long.

Part of the Hat of a Citizen is to insist the Government remains, or becomes, Legitimate.

Answer These Questions

1. Is the Government doing anything you do not agree with? (name one thing)

2. What value does that action or inaction violate?

What a Citizen Should Do

WHAT IS REQUIRED OF A CITIZEN? THIS SECTION LOOKS AT YOUR OBLIGATIONS, YOUR DUTIES.

KEY TERMS:

Patriot is a person, dictionaries seem to agree, who supports and defends his or her country. The root of the word is *patr-*, Greek and Latin for "father." Patriotism carries the sense of loving or protecting one's country as one would love and protect one's family.

Information is "a collection of facts or data" according to the *American Heritage Dictionary*. It is used to form decisions. The difficulty with information is analyzing it to "prove" its validity. *The Thinking Book* (see Further Reading) provides an excellent method of analyzing data. Decisions based on false or incomplete information are less-than-perfect. Information is needed to **vote**, to **advocate**, to **witness** or to **judge**. The word "information" comes from the Latin for "to fashion" or "to form."

Vote is, from the *American Heritage Dictionary*, "a formal expression of preference". It is also the "means by which such a preference is made known, such as a raised hand or marked ballot" and "a group of voters alike in some way: *the*

Black vote, the rural vote." The word also is used to describe the act of voting or the result of an election. It comes from the Latin, "to vow."

Witness is to say what you saw, or a person who does so. Being or performing the act of a witness can take courage. It could be said to be the defining factor of integrity. *Merriam-Webster's Dictionary of Law* specifies "one who gives evidence regarding matters of fact under inquiry; *specifically* : one who testifies or is legally qualified to testify in a case" is a witness. It comes from Old English *wit* for "mind" or "knowledge."

Advocate is the act of, or a person who does, "speak, plead or argue in favor of" something. An advocate is also a lawyer, someone who advocates the cause of another person. Advocacy, according to the *American Heritage Dictionary*, is "the act of pleading or arguing in favor of something, such as a cause, idea, or policy; active support." The word is from *vocare*, "to call."

Jury is a body of persons that **judge**, or the act of judging by such a jury. From the *American Heritage Dictionary*, a jury is "summoned by law and sworn to hear and hand down a **verdict** upon a case presented in court." It is from the Latin *jur-*or *jus*, "law" or "right."

Judge is to "form an opinion or estimation of after careful consideration" in the *American Heritage Dictionary*. A "judgement" is the opinion or estimation so formed. It comes from the Latin *jus*, "law" or "right" and *dicere*, "to decide" or "to say".

Verdict is an expressed judgment of a jury, or anything analogous: an "expressed conclusion; a judgment or opinion: *the verdict of history*" according to the *American Heritage Dictionary*. It comes from Latin for "true" + "saying."

Citizen Duties

The first act of a citizen and his last act will be to love his community, his city, state, or country. He is a patriot. It might show up as rooting for the home team, but it can also be voting in an election or serving on a jury or going to battle against terrorists. In any case, it is done because the Citizen wants the Best for his compatriots.

Below are listed a few "duties." If you do not feel competent to fulfill one or another of those duties, it is your duty to decline it. Any time the citizen is going to act on behalf of his community, his action will be based on a decision. The decision will be based on information. The first duty of a citizen is to gather and analyze information.

Gather and Analyze Information

Gathering information used to be difficult because there were too few sources. Today, we have the opposite problem. Information comes from many sources, often conflicting.

In gathering data, it is important to verify at least a few facts from any source before trusting that source. For instance, if XYZ News consistently reports things that are not true, cancel your subscription. It is also recommended, for instance, that you verify some of the facts presented in this Citizen Hat – can you trust this Hat as a source? To effectively gather information, you cannot be accepting information from any and all sources. You will drown. Verifying data as valid will prove some sources untrustworthy.

Information that has been gathered must then be analyzed. Does it make sense? Is it logical? The Thinking Book in "Further Reading" lists the exact ways that information becomes illogical (called the "illogics").

According to the book, there are about a dozen illogics, such as "contrary facts" (one source says the meeting was in Rome, another says if was in San Francisco – well, which was it?). Another is "omitted data" (the envelope is addressed to James Jones, Chicago, but has no street address). Any information containing one of the illogics will be unusable.

On the other hand, if the information you are looking at passes all the tests, it is "logical" and can be used. This analysis is extremely helpful in verifying sources. A source that consistently spews illogics need not be listened to. A citizen must be able to analyze data and make a decision based on it.

Vote

The decision can be used to vote in an election. An uninformed vote is worse than no vote at all because it is cast without regard for the effect it will have on the community. It is cast for some reason other than wanting the best for the community.

Some insist that the act of voting is more important than an informed vote. That view comes from one or the other of two ideas. First is the idea that no one knows, nor can anyone ever know, what constitutes Good Governance. Second is the desire to tear down the existing power structure.

The idea that Good Governance is unknowable comes from the works (interpreted correctly or not) of folks such as German social theorist and philosopher Jürgen Habermas whose work traces back to philosopher Kant and social theorist Marx. The essence of the argument is that "non-oppressive" society and government will come about through more and more communication.

That is undeniably true, but the argument continues: Therefore, all communication (even that from the village idiot) is as valid as any other. Therefore, an uninformed vote is as valid as an informed one. That can only be true if all communication has equal validity and that can only be true if no information is more valid than any other.

Let's test that theory.

Let us take the communication / information that "a red light means to stop." That is one datum. We also have the datum, "a red light means keep going." Is one of those data more valuable that another?

Yes. One will get you killed.

Are all data equal?

If data are unequal, then communication will be unequal. If a person is willing to accept the "information" that there is no danger in running a red light, that person believes there is no correct way to drive. He believes that a "Good Governance of

Driving" is unknowable.

Good Governance is not widely known as a subject, but that does not mean it is unknowable. An informed vote is more valuable than an uninformed one.

A proven method of tearing down an existing power structure has been to expand the "political population" (those who vote).

The Roman Monarchy used this method to become the Roman Republic 2500 years ago. At that time, tribal squabbles and vendettas were destroying the Roman Monarchy. Simply put, the power structure of the monarchy was tribal affiliation, represented by tribal elders in the Senate (*sen-*, old, an elder).

It was decided that for Rome to survive, the Monarchy had to be replaced. It was replaced by the Roman Republic, ruled by elected consuls, tribunes and various assemblies. Soldiers voted for their representatives, poor people (plebes, plebeians) voted for theirs, rich folks (patricians) for theirs. Power was no longer in the tribes but in the patricians, the soldiers, the plebes, no matter what tribe. By increasing the "political population," the power of tribal affiliation was "torn down" and transferred to new groups.

This principal of Governance (increase the political population to change the existing power structure) is so demonstrable, it could almost be said to be a Natural Law. People obey it without even knowing it.

For instance, the decade from 1961 to 1971 was a period of social upheaval in the United States, first the

Civil Rights movement and then the Anti-War movement. It was a time of great outcry to change the existing power structure. During that decade, the US Constitution was amended three times to increase the political population. Another demonstration is in the US presidential elections of 2000 and 2004. After GW Bush won in 2000, many of his opponents claimed he was not legitimate because, among other arguments, he did not win a majority of the popular vote.

The desire to increase the political population from the 538 in the Electoral College to the millions in the popular vote is rooted in a desire to "tear down an existing power structure." In 2004, GW Bush won again, this time with a majority of the popular vote. Some of his opponents claimed that he was illegitimate because not everyone voted, for whatever reason. The reasons may have been valid or not, that is not the point. The point is that those who forwarded the argument were instinctively following the principle: expand the political population to change who or what is in power.

Continued outcries against the constitutional Electoral system continue for those who want to tear down the "existing power structure."

It is an important duty to vote; more votes may tear down an existing power structure. Sometimes a power structure needs to be torn down. Good or bad, that is the value of an uninformed vote.

Witness

Another duty of a citizen is to inform others, otherwise known as "witness." Specifically, if a person has seen a crime, he has a duty to report it to the police. If he witnesses the police commit a crime, he has a duty, no matter the consequences, to report the crime to any agency that will listen.

If a citizen knows of corruption, he has a duty to be a "whistleblower" and report it. Or if you know any vital bit of information that others need in order to make an informed choice, it is your duty to let that information be known to the best of your duty. Your compatriots trust you to keep them informed. You need them to keep you informed too.

Advocate

It may or may not be a duty to advocate causes, but if a citizen sees clearly that the community should adopt certain policies, or, for its own survival, needs to take certain actions, it becomes more that a "responsibility" to advocate that cause. The later section on the "Tools (Rights) of a Citizen" will cover more fully some of the ways a citizen can effectively advocate a cause he believes in.

Judge

A final duty of a citizen is to act as a juror. Just because the police have arrested someone and the government thinks he is guilty, they are only acting on your behalf. It is your duty to determine if the police and prosecutors are truly acting for you. They have to present the evidence to you. You, informed by them and the defense as well, decide if the accused person is guilty and what his punishment should be. If he is guilty, you have a duty to your fellow citizens, in what is the Best for all, to keep the rapist off the street. If he is innocent, the next one the cops drag off the street may be you. For the safety for the community, he accused needs to be freed.

A person has many hats, but the first and final duty of a Citizen is to act in the best interests of his compatriots.

Answer These Questions

1. Name a source of information that you trust.

2. Have you ever verified any information that it gave you? Did the information turn out to be accurate? Was it complete?

3. Would you like to be more competent so you can fulfill your duties better?

Tools (Rights) of a Citizen

WHAT CAN A CITIZEN DO? THIS IS WRITTEN IN THE UNITED STATES AT THE BEGINNING OF THE 21ST CENTURY. SPECIFIC PRACTICES MAY CHANGE, BUT BASIC PRINCIPLES REMAIN THE SAME.

KEY TERMS:

Assembly is a "group of persons gathered together for a common reason, as for a legislative, religious, educational, or social purpose" says the *American Heritage Dictionary*. It is any gathering of people. From the Latin *simul*, "together."

Petition is to make "a formal written request ... to an official person or body (as a court or board)" or it is the request so made, according to the *Merriam-Webster's Dictionary of Law*. From the Latin *"to request."*

"Advocacy Group" is a group of people who advocate either for (1) a particular group or for (2) a particular policy. Examples of (1) a particular group might be senior citizens, government workers, or petroleum producing corporations. Examples of (2) a particular policy might be for the environment, against the death penalty, or to cut government spending. An advocacy group openly campaigns for its cause. Some groups, such as churches, advocate their principles, rarely deal in public policy and do not try to influence elections. Other groups exist, as their sole purpose, to influence public policy. They represent a **constituency** and will generally (U.S., 2010) set up one or more **PAC**s and engage in **lobbying**. When a group hides its actions or intent, politics becomes "dirty."

Constituency is "a body of voters represented by an officeholder" according to *The New Lexicon Webster's Dictionary*.

PAC (U.S., 2010) is a "Political Action Committee." PACs are organized under section 527 of the U.S. Internal Revenue Code and are therefore also known as "527 groups." "Most PACs," according to **www.opensecrets.org,** "represent business, such as the Microsoft PAC; labor, such as the Teamsters PAC; or ideological interests, such as the EMILY's List PAC or the National Rifle Association PAC. An organization's PAC will collect money from the group's employees or members and make contributions in the name of the PAC to candidates and political parties." Contributions can be either "**soft money**" or "**hard money**."

"Soft money" (U.S., 2010) is spent "on voter mobilization efforts and so-called issue ads," says **www.opensecrets.org**. The "so-called issue ads" will often mention candidates and their records "just before an election in a not-so-subtle effort to influence the election's outcome." This makes them an underhanded attempt to get around limits imposed by law on "**hard money**." The *American Heritage Dictionary* defines soft money as "Political donations made in such a way as to avoid federal regulations or limits, as by donating to a party organization rather than to a particular candidate or campaign."

"**Hard money**" (U.S., 2010) is "contributions for the express purpose of electing or defeating candidates." Campaign finance laws limit the amounts of "hard" money that an individual or group can give to a candidate.

"**Special Interest**" is another word for **constituency**. If the speaker likes a group, it is a "constituency" but if the group is not liked, it is a "special interest." According to the *American Heritage Dictionary*, it is "a person, group, or organization attempting to influence legislators in favor of one particular interest or issue." Any PAC or Advocacy group involved in political action, represents some special interest (constituency). Politics becomes "dirty" when actions or interests are hidden.

Lobbying comes from "lobby" which is a "public room next to the assembly chamber of a legislative body" says the *American Heritage Dictionary*. Lobbyists used to stand around in the lobby of a legislative chamber and grab legislators and they came and went from their meetings.

Lobbying is working to "influence the thinking of legislators or other public officials for or against a specific cause." There are law firms and other companies that will use their contacts to lobby for a fee. They provide a service to **Advocacy groups** and **PACs** and, one would suppose, individuals who wish to **petition** the government.

FOIA (U.S., 2010) is the abbreviation of the "Freedom of Information Act" which became law in 1966. The U.S. Congress, in the FOIA, declared any Federal government agency is required to provide the public with information about its activities and data at its disposal. It allows "any person" to make an FOIA request and, as long as the information does not fall under certain exceptions, such as an ongoing criminal investigation, the agency is duty-bound to provide it. FIOA has led to similar "Sunshine Laws" in many states and even other countries.

Making the Government Obey

As said in the introduction to this Hat, "For most of history in most parts of the world, the job of a Citizen was to obey. The people were owned by the government . . ."

Those of us living in what is called a "Western Democracy" instinctively sense that we are responsible for our own situations and that we own the government. Yet we are constantly told, and many have come to believe, that "special interests," whether they be "multinational corporate interests" or "environmentalist whackos," own the government and we do not.

That sentiment is borne out in our own experience. Did you ever write to your Congressman and get a form letter back? Receiving that non-answer, you get the idea that you are not being listened to and therefore those who scream "special interests!" make sense. Those interests, it is said, have special access to lawmakers. You look in the mirror and ask, "What can one citizen do?"

You Can Fight City Hall

Everyone knows you can't fight City Hall. Surely, whoever originated that "truism" worked in City Hall. Some people in City Hall would prefer to run the government without *you* rocking the boat.

Consider, for instance, the top brass of a government workers union -- which is not to say that *all* honchos in any union of bureaucrats desires to control the population, but you can see that some might. Such a person, whether the boss of a labor union, CEO of an oil company, or a so-called "poverty pimp" (one whose power is based on keeping people dependant on government) has no more right to control the government than you do. He may have *more* access, but he has no *special* access.

In the United States, what gives him access is the Constitution. The Constitution provides *anyone* the tools to make the government obey, if he will only use them. At the time the Constitution was written, these tools were so well known, they were thought too obvious to mention. But for the new government to be ratified, it was demanded the Constitution be amended to clarify these rights (tools) of the people.

The First Amendment guarantees six rights. The first three rights (establishment of religion, exercise of religion, speech) are the cornerstones of Jeffersonian Democracy, named for Thomas Jefferson, the author of the Declaration of Independence. This is the democracy of the responsible individual speaking his mind. As James Madison said in The Federalist Papers, "if men were angels" no government would be necessary. In fact, if men were angels, the above three rights would *be* the government. Everywhere, each individual would do what he knew was right and have no fear to announce it. If men were angels, a Benign Anarchy would reign.

However, men are not angels. Jeffersonian

rights *alone* are not sufficient to make the government obey. Yet they, almost exclusively, are what we learn of "rights" in school. Ponder a moment why that might be. (Why would, say, an antisocial person in charge of the curriculum of a school want to emphasis only those rights that are *not* sufficient to make the government obey?)

Madisonian Democracy

The final three rights of the First Amendment (press, assembly, and petition) are the cornerstones of Madisonian Democracy, named for James Madison, the author of the First Amendment.

This is the democracy in which you and I, having some grievance against the government, may widely announce our view in the "press," may gather like-minded individuals to our cause, assemble with them and then petition the government to correct the error. And if our representatives do not heed us, and there are enough of us, we can turn them out of office. That depends on you and me agreeing that we have a common interest. Madison wrote of "factions" (see Federalist number 10), which are "a number of citizens . . . united and actuated by some common . . . interest. . . ." You have "common interest" with a number of "factions." You may be a dairy farmer, or a member of a religion, or a parent. You may be all three, in which case you have three "interests."

You have been taught, of course, that special interests are bad, and if, heaven forbid, you found yourself as a part of a special interest, you are an oppressor. The design of such propaganda is to ensure you do not participate. It is antisocial hogwash. Before you buy it, ask, "who benefits from my non-participation?" The obvious answer is, "those who now have access." They do not want you to dilute their influence. (See "What A Citizen Does" above – expanding the political population upsets the current power structure.)

As long as others can make you believe "politics is dirty" and keep you out of the process, they control the process. They become "City Hall" but you *can* fight that. Perhaps the simplest way is to find a group advocating your interest.

When you find such a group, participate in it. When you participate, you become more than you are.

Advocacy groups exist for almost any interest. You may contribute to and participate at any level – from making an occasional donation to holding an office. You may contribute or join as many groups as you like. Advocacy groups often use "Sunshine Laws" (such as the FOIA) to find out what is really going on in government. An individual may use these laws as well. Few know, for instance, that the CAFR (Comprehensive Annual Financial Report) of most governments exists, is available, and can be *very* revelatory as to where the government gets its money and where it is *really* spent.

Advocacy Groups (PACs)

The "special interests" did not change Washington in a day. Some have spent decades. The Education Establishment has spent over 100 years getting us to where we are now. (See *The Leipzig*

Connection in **Further Reading**). Most Advocacy groups that aim at affecting public policy will sponsor one or more Political Action Committees (PACs). A PAC often will hire a lobbyist. The lobbyist finds elected officials who agree with the positions of the Advocacy group, those who oppose it, and legislation that will affect the interests of the group. The Advocacy group uses information about legislation to launch campaigns to educate the public about the issues and the positions. The PAC works with the lobbyist to keep in office (and even help gain higher office) those officials who agree with the group's positions, and defeat those who oppose their positions.

What about that form letter from your Congressman? Your congressman represents over 600,000 individuals as of 2005 (700,000+ by 2017), not to mention countless groups. *Every one of them wants access.* Elected representatives and their staffs are communication magnets. Phone calls, emails and Faxes pour in daily. The Congressman and his staff are constantly barraged with "vote for this" -- "vote against that" -- "support this" -- "oppose that" -- and, oh, yes, there is your letter, too.

Not only that, but also, when the official is working, he has to stay informed on a thousand subjects, attend hearings and meetings and fundraising and campaign functions so he can keep his job. When the representative is not "working," he is back in his district, shaking hands and attending town hall meetings, community events, and, of course fundraising and campaign functions so he can keep his job. His Chief-of-Staff helps organize his schedule.

Family? There is a constant tug-of-war between staff and family members. The result is *overload* for both elected official and staff members. To cope, they devise a system to prioritize. The most important communications go to the elected official, next most important to the Chief of Staff, then down the ranks to staff assistants and finally Interns, who crank out form letters. The elected official cannot read every letter.

Greg Mitchell, years a Chief of Staff to a US Congressman, says there is a "pecking order" who a Congressman listens to. Assuming the Congressman's expertise is in tax law, he may not know how to vote on, for instance, an Education measure. Who will the representative listen to?

- Family
- Long-time Friend
- Close Colleague
- Advocacy Group who is Big Fundraiser
- Expert who is Donor
- Big Donors
- Big Companies
- Mid-level Donors
- Tallies of letters for and against

Not surprising, the top of the list is family and close friends. If the spouse or a long-time friend is an educator, the official will ask advice.

Next are colleagues. When a vote comes up on an education bill, he'll get advice from a colleague on the Education committee. He will also listen to an Education Advocacy group that is a *big fundraiser*. The group supports him because he agrees with their positions. Therefore someone from that group will give him advice consistent with his own positions. Next comes Industry "experts" who are *donors*, and the *biggest individual donors*, and large groups that can deliver votes back home. Finally, the representative will listen to big companies back home and *mid-level* donors. Of course, he listens to you, too. As the Intern sent out form letters, he tallied how many constituents supported the education bill and how many opposed it.

Right or wrong, these elected officials have to cope with their overload and somehow stay in office too. The above is how they do it. If you want access, you have to work *with* them and their situation. As Greg Mitchell explains, "Who has access? It is simple. They just don't have enough time to meet with, truly listen to, and learn from regular people and groups who do not help them survive in office. Those who help them, get their time, their attention and their help."

YOU have Access

Some say only "special interests" have access. That is not true, but as an individual, you will have a difficult time even locating which elected officials agree with your interests, let alone electioneer and raise funds and donate to every one of them. But as a member of an advocacy group, your interests *can* be represented effectively. The group's PAC will hire a lobbyist. The lobbyist will find the representatives who agree with your interest. The PAC will work with them to keep them in office. You can participate as much or as little as you want, and yet your interests are being advocated. *You* have access, through your group.

As a Citizen, you have a right to have your interests represented in government. You do not have a right to have your interest represented *effectively*, but through an Advocacy group that agrees with you, you can have access and effective representation.

To sum up, what are your options to change the government?

Option 1: Riot and shoot police and demand everything be torn down. Got to jail or get shot.

Option 2: Stand on your "rights" as you see them, listen to no one else, demand to be heard. You will be heard, convince no one and be ignored.

Option 3: Work with others to gain access, make the changes you want, fix the system. Not as heroic as 1 or 2, not as sexy, may not work next week. But steady application will get the job done.

Answer These Questions

1. What specifically do you want to change in the government?

2. Are there other people who want the same thing?

3. Other groups?

4. What would happen if you participated or contributed to one of those groups?

After all that ...
What can you do to Keep the Republic?

Further Reading

THE CITIZEN HAT ABOVE IS A START.

A search of the Internet will undoubtedly find you a selection of Advocacy groups that espouse one or more of your interests. You will have to decide which one(s) best represent you.

While you are becoming active, the following will increase your understanding. You will also find other materials on your own.

http://www.ItsYourConstitution.com is the website of the author of this little book. Come on by, see what's cooking!

The Destiny of Freedom: *A Manual for the American Citizen* by Daniel Leacox & Donald Seyfried, ISBN 096786770-3. Out-of-print and difficult to find. If you can find it, it is an excellent companion to this volume. Chapter by chapter, doing the exercises at the end of each, a person gains a practical understanding of what a Citizen can do to keep his Freedom.

The Constitution of the United States*: A Study Guide* by John Chambers. Do the exercises and answer the questions at the end of each section. As the back cover says: "when you complete this book, you will have read and understood the entire U.S. Constitution." ISBN 1-928729-06-1

The Federalist Papers is the name given to 85 newspaper articles written in 1787-88 by

"Publius" (penname of James Madison, Alexander Hamilton and John Jay) urging the people of the 13 American states to adopt the proposed constitution and become The United States. The articles are a wealth of information on Good Governance. They are available in various books in most any public library and on many websites.

The Anti-Federalist Papers and the Constitutional Convention Debates edited by Ralph Ketcham, ISBN 0-451-62525-0 gives other sides to the debate over adopting the US Constitution, also providing lessons in Good Governance.

http://www.constitution.org has an extensive library of books, documents and blogs related to the U.S. Constitution and the subject of Good Governance. Many of the materials on these pages may be found on this web site.

Polybius (c.203-122 BCE), Greek historian at the time of the Roman Republic, gives important lessons on the subject of Good Governance. He observed three basic forms of government and how these forms cycle from one to the next. In the cycle, he "enumerate[d] six forms of government, --the three commonly spoken of which I have just mentioned, and three more allied forms, I mean *despotism, oligarchy* and *mob-rule.*" That is, three forms of government and each one's evil twin brother. His works can be found in public libraries and on many websites. A later refinement, usually attributed to Alexander Fraser Tytler (Lord Woodhouselee), a Scottish historian of the late 18th century describes the cycle in greater detail. With minor variations, it is generally quoted as:

> A democracy cannot exist as a permanent form of government. It can only exist until the voters discover that they can vote themselves largesse from the public treasury. From that moment on, the majority always votes for the candidates promising the most benefits from the public treasury with the result that a democracy always collapses over loose fiscal policy, always followed by a dictatorship.

> The average age of the world's greatest civilizations has been 200 years. . . . The people progress from bondage to spiritual faith; from spiritual faith to great courage; from courage to liberty; from liberty to abundance; from abundance to selfishness; from selfishness to complacency; from complacency to apathy; from apathy to dependency; from dependency back again to bondage."

http://duke.usask.ca/~porterj/DeptTransls/Polybius.html is a readable translation of Polybius

Basic American Government by Clarence B. Carson, American Textbook Committee, Wadley, Alabama (1995) "gives an account of the general government as established by the Constitution...." It looks into the "ancient and modern foundations, scriptural and secular" and then gives "a sobering description of the massive departures from the Constitution in the 20th century." As a history, it emphasizes the contributions of religious and spiritual thought.

The Leipzig Connection: *The Systematic Destruction of American Education* by Paolo Lionni, ISBN 0-89739-001-6. American Education has been being undermined for over 100 years. Easy to read, but it gives you the scorecard so you know the players and how they worked together. Almost reads like a detective story.

For Good and Evil: The Impact of Taxes on the Course of Civilization by Charles Adams, ISBN 1-56833-024-3. The title says it all.

"The Antisocial Personality" and **"The Social Personality"** by L. Ron Hubbard has bogus copies around the internet. (Don't believe everything you see!)) Use this: **http://www.scientologyhandbook.org/suppression /SH11_1.HTM**

The Thinking Book based on the works of L. Ron Hubbard, ISBN 0897390113. "How do you sort through a volume of confusing and conflicting data to arrive at truth? Trying to state what is truth has proved difficult so Hubbard took a different approach." His approach is to systematically analyze the data for false or incomplete "facts," compartment them and discern whose data can be trusted.

Democracy in America by Alexis de Tocqueville (written in 1831-32) describes the experience of America and why it worked compared to governmental systems in Europe at the time. A classic in the subject of Governance.

The Oxford History of the American People by Samuel Eliot Morison. A set of volumes, this is one to check out of a public library and study carefully.

And beyond ...

www.ingramcontent.com/pod-product-compliance
Lightning Source LLC
Chambersburg PA
CBHW050053260726
48658CB00005B/1927